My Life & Times at Doomadgee

Maree Manly

Copyright

By Maree Manly © Copyright 2020
All rights reserved.
Book Layout Interior and Cover ©2020 - EvolveGlobalPublishing.com

This book is privately published and cannot be sold or re-distributed.

No part of this book may be reproduced or transmitted in any form or by any means, electronic or mechanical, including photocopying, recording or by any information storage and retrieval system.

The information contained in this book is for information purposes only, and may not apply to your situation. The author provides no warranty about the content or accuracy of content enclosed. The information provided is subjective. Keep this in mind when reading this book. The Author shall be not be liable for any loss of profit or any other commercial damages resulting from the use of this book.

People of Aboriginal/Islander descent are warned that this book might contain images of people who have died.

My Life and Times At Doomadgee Changes
1st Edition. 2020
ISBN: 978-1-64764-568-7 (Hardcover)

TRADEMARKS

All product names, logos, and brands are the property of their respective owners. All company, product, and service names used in this book are for identification purposes only. The use of these names, logos, and brands does not imply endorsement. All other trademarks cited herein are the property of their respective owners.

Special thanks to Marie Parsons, who gave me sanctuary to write my book.

To my friend and 'Sister from another mother' Patsy O'Keefe, my gratitude for allowing me to tell her story.

Edited by Lorraine Carter, without whose help this book would not have seen the light of day.

Table of Contents

ABOUT THE AUTHOR 7

MY LIFE AND TIMES IN DOOMADGEE 9

CHAPTER 1 15

CHAPTER 2 23

CHAPTER 3 37

CHAPTER 4 47

CHAPTER 5 59

CHAPTER 6 65

ABOUT THE AUTHOR

Maree Manly graduated from Queensland University as a matured aged student in 1983 with an Arts degree, majoring in anthropology/sociology encompassing Aboriginal Studies, both traditional and contemporary. While studying, Maree lived in Duchesne College for 3 years.

On leaving University, Maree was employed by the Department of Aboriginal and Islander Affairs as a Liaison Officer and assigned to the Cherbourg Aboriginal Community, where she spent 2½ years before being transferred to Doomadgee. Maree spent 7 years in Doomadgee creating the memories that she recalls in this book.

Maree has three grown children and now lives in retirement with her husband, Maxwell, in Charters Towers.

Maree Manly

MY LIFE AND TIMES IN DOOMADGEE

This is Doomadgee 1986, Christmas Day. The red dust is everywhere, it gets into places that you would not believe. It gets hot and the ground is unbearable to walk on. The dust swirls up and leaves you breathless.

The temperature is in the forties and eventually the whole community has gone down to the river to seek some respite from the oppressive heat. Clouds are forming and the black cockatoos are a sure sign of rain. Since the sighting of the black cockatoos, everyone has been looking skyward, watching for signs of the monsoon they hope will come soon. In the distance, low rumbling can heard from the west. It is hoped this is heralding soaking rains.

The local women hope the rains will come soon as it will mean that the roads will be cut in both directions, then no grog can be brought into the community. When the rains come it means peace in the community….no fighting, no drunks in the streets and more money for food, rent and other necessities. Most families have spent their money on Christmas gifts, so everyone is in the same situation, but that also means no grog or "gangi".

Doomadgee is situated on the Nicholson River, 500km north of Mt Isa, one hour by air, 9 hours by road and it is cut off from the rest of the world for three months of the year when the monsoons come. Then, the only way in is by air and the plane is not permitted to carry grog. To most of the wives and mothers, the monsoon is a blessing as they have two to three months of an almost normal community.

When the river floods, access is cut off at the Weir, but people still use boats to get across to try to get to Burketown to buy grog. Their attempts are mostly unsuccessful and they then have to be rescued by the locals.

Early housing

The housing situation consisted of shacks down by the river. They were constructed from bits and pieces of timber and corrugated iron and whatever else the people could find. On the other side of the road from the river the houses were made from timber, with corrugated iron roofs and dirt floors. There were some modern homes made from cement blocks, designed and constructed in the block-making shed in Doomadgee. This created work for the men and was a cost-saving enterprise. It was cheaper to make the bricks in Doomadgee than bring them in from Mt Isa. There was one mud-brick house which was built as an experiment, to test whether it would be a suitable design for the location. It was deemed unsuitable as it was too labour intensive. It could be looked at again as an alternative building material, especially for aged care units and single parent accommodation.

Locally made blocks

New block house under construction

The township consists of 800 people, 600 Aborigines and 200 whites who are mainly teachers, nurses, tradies and admin staff.

There is a store run by Queensland Government employees, with locals working the checkouts and filling shelves. The bakery and butchery are run by local people and there is a piggery run by a white overseer.

The school is staffed by four teachers and a principal, all white. There is no hospital, just a first-aid station run by nurses. The Flying Doctor is only a phone call away but takes 45 minutes to fly to Doomadgee.

CHAPTER 1

Maree Manly

New block ho The DC3 that Maree arrived on

The whine of the DC3's propellers became almost hypnotic. I was on my way to the Aboriginal community of Doomadgee in the Gulf Country of Queensland to take up a position as a Liaison Officer. The pilot had advised us that we would be flying at 500ft. I looked out the window and could see the tops of the trees. The plane was not pressurised, so we needed ear plugs and as we boarded the hostess had given everyone Minties to chew to prevent our ears from popping. The flight took an hour and was at times bumpy as we were flying so low. Finally, the pilot announced that we were landing in Doomadgee and as the plane circled the town, I could see lots of red dirt and a few houses.

The airstrip was constructed from termite mound soil so as we landed, the plane bumped and lunged to a halt. As we left the aircraft the heat hit us like a wave, it was almost unbearable. My first thought was, "Oh my God, where am I? This is terrible!". I looked for the Terminal, but all I could see was a tin shed, painted pink, with the word 'Doomadgee' on the side. Two vehicles were parked at the fence, and among the black folk I could see one smiling white man approaching me.

"Welcome to Doomadgee!" he said, "my name is John Keleher."

"Hi John," I replied, as he took my bags and placed them in his ute.

As we took off for town, I asked John where I would be staying.

"In a house that we have prepared for you," he replied, "it needs a few more things but you just let me know what you need and I will get it for you."

"Great!", I thought, "this is a good start. What else do they have in store for me?"

As we left the airport, I could see what looked like a shop, then an office building. We turned left and drove into a driveway.

"Home, sweet home!" John joked.

I looked at the house and thought, "What a dump! It must be better inside."

I opened the front door and saw that it was still a dump, full of red dust and smelling of something that I could not identify.

John brought my bags in and stood, hands on hips. "Well," he asked, "what do you think?"

I looked at him and said, "I have a question. When is the next plane out of here?"

John just laughed and said, "You will get used to it. Just give it time, it will grow on you."

"Not much chance of that!" I thought.

Then I remembered my old boss from Cherbourg saying, "Make your home a sanctuary, then, when you finish work each day, close the door and play the music you love to listen to."

I sat down on the unmade bed and my thoughts went back to Cherbourg, where all this started. I could see the faces of all the people I had worked with and cared about. Les Stewart, the Chairman, who had been so kind to this white woman who came straight from University, full of ideas and enthusiasm. Cherbourg was an aboriginal settlement that had a bad reputation, and yet I found it and its people just like every other small town. I was welcomed by everyone and I settled in and enjoyed my work and learning the history of the settlement. It had a dark, harsh past that was still remembered by the elders and was a constant reminder of what had been done to the Aboriginal people, especially the children who were taken from their parents and placed in separate dormitories, boys in one and girls in the other. I spent two years in Cherbourg and until I upset the Minister for Aboriginal Affairs, I thought I would stay there indefinitely! But, two weeks after that incident, I was on a plane to Doomadgee. This was my punishment!

I pulled myself out of my reverie and started to look around the house. "It's not so bad," I thought, "at least I am not sharing. It just needs a good clean and a bit more furniture."

Where I was going to get that I wasn't sure. Anyhow, I decided to get stuck in and make it a home!

My first day at work was a real eye-opener! I shared an office with the other Liaison Officer and we had only the Flying Doctor radio, no telephones or faxes. I had never used a radio so that was a steep learning curve! There were only certain times that we could use the radio and even then, we could be cut off at any time.

I started to enjoy listening to the conversations between the doctors, the patients and the station owners who took the opportunity to catch up with neighbours who could be hundreds of kilometres away. It gave me an insight into just how isolated Doomadgee was!

I was visited by locals who were curious to see the new Liaison Officer and I was always made welcome.

Doomadgee had been run for forty-three years by the Exclusive Brethren, originally the Plymouth Brethren who came down through the Gulf to Doomadgee. They established the mission with the help of the Queensland Government. They quickly took over all aspects of the lives of the aboriginal people. Men and women were sent out to stations to work, children were put in girls' and boys' dormitories. The only ones left in the community were the older men and women and the missionaries.

Life under the missionaries was harsh and controlled. It was aimed at keeping everyone abiding by the rules! The children were the ones who suffered the most, as sometimes they only saw their parents once a year. The parents' wages were kept by the missionaries and doled out in dribs and drabs. If the missionaries purchased clothing for the residents, such as jeans, shirts or dresses, that amount was deducted from their wages. They were not allowed to buy their own clothes or gear.

It was a closed community, as far as the missionaries were concerned and there were strict rules. No tobacco, no music, no grog, and the locals had to get permission to do anything from marrying to how much money they were allowed.

As far as I can determine, the missionaries were not consciously mean to the people, it was their belief that they were 'saving' the aborigines from their devilish and heathen ways! This seems to be the mantra of all missionaries, no matter what part of the world they went to. They do not see that they destroy cultures that are thousands of years old, yet Christianity is only 2,000 years old. The missionaries in Lockhart River mission were asked by the people if they could bring their totem poles in to put in a museum but they were refused, then the totem poles piled up and burnt.

The pastor, who is still in Doomadgee today, had his own home with everything technical long before the community had air-conditioning. He and his wife wielded such power over the people, it was frightening to see that the couple had such control over the people in the community.

CHAPTER 2

When the Department of Aboriginal Affairs took over in 1983 after the missionaries left, they had to start from scratch with everything. The missionaries had controlled the wages of those who went to work on the stations, and that along with workers' compensation payments, child endowment, tax refunds, were kept in bank books in the names of residents while the owners were unaware that they existed. The child endowment meant for the parents had been taken from them by the missionaries for looking after the children. The bank books were found under a desk in my office. After we contacted the Public Trustee it was eventually sorted out, but the missionaries should never have had that sort of power. It makes you wonder what happened in other missions, all done in the name of God! It was a lot for me to take in as I had never dealt with missionaries before and I was shocked to find out how bad it was. Compensation for death or injury from accidents, or unpaid wages on stations had not been applied for or paid.

Residents came into my office to ask permission to leave the community and I advised them that they did not have to do that any longer, as they were free to come and go as they wished! After 43 years of asking permission, it was hard for them to understand that they were now free to make their own decisions.

The Doomadgee Council had been formed to take some of the responsibility for running the community, but the Department had the last say on everything. They just replaced the missionaries!

Life did get better for the people when CDEP (Community Development Employment Projects) was introduced as work for the dole. Men and women could stay in the community and look after their own children and the elders. It was so great to see people coming to work each morning! I have never forgotten an incident that happened one morning I as walking to work. It was August, and a heavy fog hung in the air. The Council and CDEP workers passed on their way to their jobs. They were talking and laughing and skylarking as they came out of the fog. Yet another photo I neglected to take but it is stored in my memory. It gives me joy to remember such times.

We were looking forward to getting Telstra service – we already had intermittent ABC radio reception and some television from Darwin, though the sunspot activity interrupted the radio so some days we had no news. When TV and telephone finally arrived, the isolation did not seem so all-encompassing!

Phone comes to Doomadgee

The heat was about to come with a vengeance, after the cool and sometimes cold of the winter it was hard to take. These were the days before air-conditioning, we only had fans. When I look back now, I cannot believe that I lived through fifty degree days! One Christmas, it was fifty-two degrees and we all went and sat in the river.

Talking about the river, it was my saviour in more ways than one. I fished from it, sat in it, swam in it and put pots in to catch redclaw. I especially enjoyed watching the fresh water come down. After weeks of no water, then, like a miracle, it suddenly roared down and was full. The whole community would run down to see the spectacle!

Doomadgee was surrounded by a lot of places to visit, such as Escott Station, Lawn Hill, Adels Grove, Gregory Downs, Old Doomadgee and Burketown. They were all part of the adventure, in spite of the condition of the roads! There were also plenty of places to camp and there was always an abundance of fish and crabs. The Hells Gate Roadhouse was also very popular with residents and travellers, good for a feed and drinks.

I settled into the life in a remote community, 500km from Mt Isa. You get used to the heat and adjust your life and work accordingly. When we finally got air-conditioning, we could not believe how we managed without it! As for telephones, it was a great day when we made our last call on the Flying Doctor radio, although I missed the daily chatter. Strangely enough, I felt more isolated. Having the telephones made my job easier, but I lost the joy of communicating with the surrounding stations.

Life changed in Doomadgee as the people had a purpose in working for the benefit of the community. CDEP workers were employed at the Hospital, the school and the store. Husbands and wives were employed, and each had their own money, which was a huge change from life under the missionaries when the women were not allowed to have bank accounts.

Some elders believed that it was good when the missionaries were in Doomadgee, but that was because, after they left, drugs and alcohol were introduced and there was no longer the regimented lifestyle that the people were used to.

One side effect of the missionaries' beliefs was that the church Pastor married everyone, not taking into account whether they were cousins or close kin. This caused a lot of concern among the elders who still practised the old ways, such as who married whom. The missionaries banned all traditional languages and ceremonies, so the people developed a hand/eye form of communication which was used when they didn't want the missionaries to know what they were saying. Even though traditional song and dance was banned, the people still practised them in secret. This was especially true of languages which were spoken within families. Dr David Trigger, from the University of Queensland spent some time recording the languages of each household.

There was a resident 'Medicine man" named Blue Bob, who, despite the missionaries, tended to all sorts of maladies. He was not averse to sending people to the white doctors though. Traditional medicine was very much a part of the lives of the people of Doomadgee. Some of the traditional medicines were from local trees and plants, such as the water lily bulbs and the fruit and leaves of the Tamarind tree. Leaves from one tree were crushed and thrown into the river to stun the fish, making them an easy catch.

Food from wildlife played an important part in the lives of the people. Kangaroo and fish were especially popular, and crabbing produced a real treat. If anyone caught fish, it was always shared with the elders who were given first preference. Elders were always looked after in that sense. The older women still went out to get sugar bag, wild honey and other bush tucker. They followed traditional ways such as cooking underground with paperbark and hot coals, called Kup-Murri. I have eaten many a meal cooked by the women this way, an art that you don't learn overnight. These women knew how to do it as they had been taught by their mothers and grandmothers. While down by the river or out camping, the women cooked meat and vegetables underground and these were some of the most delicious meals I ever tasted!

Local women cooking underground

The women would collect Kangaroo grasses and then spend hours rolling the blades on their thighs to bind the grass together. It was then soaked to stain it, using various natural dyes made from leaves etc in water. Using intricate patterns, the women then wove the grass into bags. They also made mats and hats from Pandanus leaves. These skills were passed on to daughters and young ones who were interested, preserving their ancestral ways for future generations. To see the women sitting cross-legged in under a tree, making bags, talking and laughing was a wonderful sight to watch. It was as if time had stood still.

Woven bags and shield

Local women weaving

The men made didgeridoos and shields, and I noticed that they were now doing ceremonies such as corroborees and dances, while the women had their songs and dances which they passed on to their children, especially the girls. The elder women, aunts and grandmothers, were in charge of all aspects of the girls' lives, from menstruation to marriage and birthing, and passing on the traditions in the women's lives. Mt Isa Health workers tried to arrange workshops on women's and girl's health, but this upset the elders who had always been in charge of this area of 'women's business'. The workshops were cancelled!

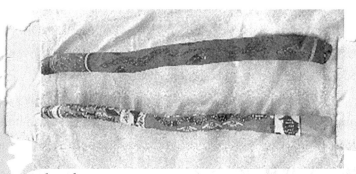

Didgeridoos

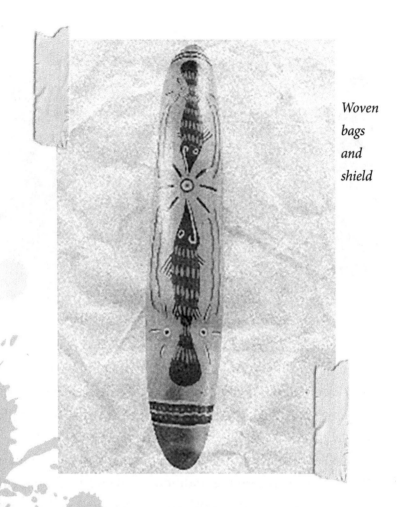

Woven bags and shield

Even though their culture was suppressed, it was driven underground and still practised. It goes to show how strong Aboriginal culture is, no matter what their background!

When I first arrived, there were no Police stationed in Doomadgee, the nearest were in Burketown, 95kms away. They came over if they were needed. Over the years, a Police station and residence were built and Police were finally stationed at Doomadgee. It gave the residents some feelings of security knowing that the Police were on hand if needed. The relationship between the Police and the community was fragile at times, it depended on who the Police were and whether they wanted to be stationed in Doomadgee and enjoy their time there.

Doomadgee Police

Doomadgee Police bogged on the Boorooloola Road

The Blue Light Discos run by the Police for the children were popular. The Aboriginal Police were the only form of policing in the early days and they continue to do this role today! The men and women doing this job always felt that they were contributing to the community and it gave them status. It was never an easy job, especially when their own families were involved. They were always kind to and protective of me in all my dealings with them, especially Freddy O'Keefe who was an aboriginal Police officer. Freddy was very supportive of me in my role as a Liaison Officer.

Police Troopy

Doomadgee Ambulance

When I arrived in Doomadgee in 1986, the Aboriginal Health team were dynamic and enthusiastic. Nothing was too much trouble and they were keen to improve the health of the community. They visited the school and people in their homes, especially the elderly and mothers with babies. They held workshops and encouraged healthy eating and lifestyles. Then it all changed when the hierarchy in Mt Isa decided to change the roles of the teams. They went from a team who went out into the community to a team that could only see people in their office. Now, anyone who knows aboriginal people well would know that they hate going to what they see as 'white man's offices'. They felt that the team was no longer there to look after them as they had in the past. The members of the team were disappointed in these changes in their roles.

Life in Doomadgee was busy and challenging every day, especially for me as it was more remote than where I had previously lived. The isolation got to me sometimes, especially when the heat was at its height. The plane came in twice a week with passengers, goods and mail. The mail plane was always welcome, and everyone went to the airport to see what it would bring! Visitors were always welcome too and it was great to hear what was happening in the world outside of Doomadgee! I looked forward to receiving the newspapers, even though they were almost a week late!

One special visitor who was very welcome was the Governor of Queensland, Leneen Ford, a Canadian who had made Australia her home. The days before the Governor arrived were busy, getting all the arrangements sorted out for her arrival. I had suggested to the Chairman of Council, Wilfred Walden, that we put on billy tea and damper, as I thought the Governor would appreciate having what we have over an open fire when we go camping. It would be a novelty!

The Governor arrived and was greeted by the Council and community. The chairman swung the billy around in the air and totally impressed the Governor, who stated that she had never had such a good cup of tea, served with such flair! The damper was made by one of the older women and was so good that there were only crumbs left. The Governor was then taken on a tour of the community and was a delightful visitor who appreciated the problems facing aboriginal people in remote areas such as Doomadgee. It was great to have such an interesting visitor who compared the plight of the aborigines to the First Nation Canadian Indians.

Not all visitors to Doomadgee were as kind or as helpful as Governor Ford. One of those was a journalist called Heather Brown from the Australian Newspaper, who came under the guise of writing an upbeat article about life in Doomadgee. We waited with anticipation for the newspaper to arrive! When it finally came, (remember we only received mail twice a week), to say that we were shocked is an understatement! The article took up a whole page, with the title in capital letters, DOOMCITY! The Chairman, Wilfred Walden was so upset as he had made Heather Brown welcome and thought she would write something positive. Instead, she wrote a devastating description of life in Doomadgee that shocked us all, and still resonates today. Mention Doom City to anyone from Doomadgee and you will see the effect it had on the whole community. It was sad to see a community go into mourning over a newspaper article. The people were ashamed to have their home portrayed in such a way in a National newspaper. It was equivalent to the article about Palm Island being the most dangerous place on earth. People who write these destructive articles should come visit and see the effect their work has on a whole community for years to come.

My life and work in Doomadgee was always rewarding but sometimes lonely so I chose a puppy for company. Her mother was part dingo and father was German Shepherd, so I thought she would be great company. I had to wait till she was weaned to pick her up, which was about 5 weeks. When I finally got her home, I was mesmerised by her antics as she chased lizards, moths and flies! She was such good company that I was glad to see her every day when I came home. It wasn't long before she was climbing my 6ft high fence to follow me to work, so I had to put her on a run which stopped the climbing. She loved to climb onto my waterbed, which ended in disaster when she put a hole in the bladder. Imagine the mess! It was lucky my house was high set, the water just ran down through the floor, not into the rest of the house.

As you can imagine, life was not always happy. There were times and events that made me sad and feeling isolated, especially during holidays, however I was determined to make my time in Doomadgee mean something. I applied to Council to run the Aged Persons Hostel, which housed about 10 elder residents aged from late 30s to 100. This job gave me great satisfaction, as the residents taught me patience and understanding.

A special resident, and the oldest in the Hostel was Lizzie Daylight. Lizzie tried to teach me language, but I was a sorry student. Lizzie would cackle at my awful attempts at everyday language. She was a delight to have in the Hostel, until some nights after dark. It was always a full moon or a starlit night when I would hear Lizzie yelling in language at top note. I would run to her room to find her under the bed with all her possessions, crying. From what I could gather from her broken English, she was hiding from the troopers who came on horseback to take her children. She would hide them under bushes and run so the troopers would chase her. She was terrified and made the noise of the horses with her hands on the floor under her bed, while speaking in language between sobs.

I managed to convince her that I would lock the gates so the troopers could not get into our compound! She would finally agree to come out from under the bed and would sit, shivering, on the chair next to it. Now, if these were real memories or part and parcel of dementia, I am not sure, but they were very real to Lizzie. She lived during the era of troopers hunting down Aborigines and bringing them into missions and towns. Lizzie's behaviour upset me because she was so distressed by these memories of the past.

Lizzie had a large family of 10 children. Her grandson Cameron died in a Police cell on Palm Island. I remember Cameron for the patience he showed Lizzie when he lived with her in Doomadgee. He always made her tea the way she liked it, hot and strong. Later in life she liked milk in her tea and lots of sugar, not how she was used to in the old days.

Lizzie

The old folk like Lizzie should be remembered by everyone, they are part of the history of the aboriginal people and were the keepers of their song and dance.

If there was a medical emergency in Doomadgee, it meant that the Flying Doctor had to be called from Mt Isa. If you were lucky, the plane might have been in the area meeting another emergency on one of the many properties or communities in the Gulf. The Flying Doctor played a part in my life when I became ill with a gall bladder attack. The pain was unbearable, and when the plane landed I was treated with kindness and expertise by all the crew, from the Doctor to the nurse and pilot. This service is underrated by those who have never had to use it! Living in remote areas such as the Gulf, and really the whole of Western Queensland, meant you had to rely on the Flying Doctors, sometimes in life and death situations! Mothers and babies were often passengers on these planes. The sound of the plane at all hours of the day and night was reassuring to the people, especially the doctors and nurses who live and work in remote communities. It was and still is assurance that help is on its way. The medical staff are an integral part of life in communities such as Doomadgee. Combined with the Flying Doctors, they give a service which we all should support and be proud of.

FRDS Plane

While I am on the subject of planes, during my time at Doomadgee, because the airstrip was constructed of compacted ant hill it was not an all-weather strip. It was plagued with hawks and other birds, so a bird shot gun was installed which went off every half hour. However, some birds became used to the sound and sat on the gun. When it fired, they flew off, then returned to sit on the gun again. It was quite funny to watch, and I am sorry that I never got around to taking photos! The birds always were and still are a problem which I am sure most airports experience. Of course, over the years the airstrip has been made all weather and lights installed, making it much safer for planes and helicopters to land. The Flying Doctor pilots' job would now be much easier!

Whenever my boss was away, it fell to me and the admin and council staff to light the strip when the Flying Doctor was to land at night. That involved driving a ute, with the driver's door open, dropping the tins with lighter fluid and lighting them one by one along the length of the strip. All the while, we had to watch for the blinking red and white lights and listening for the sound of the plane. The drone of the plane was always a welcome sound for all involved. When the pilot took off with the patient on board, we then had to pick up the tins, extinguish the flame and set them up for the next emergency situation.

I remember the time when I was manning the radio on a weekend and a call came in from Dick Smith, requesting permission to land to refuel his chopper. He was on his way through to the Northern Territory. I checked that there was enough Avgas and set it up ready for his arrival. He landed and we set up the drums and refuelled his chopper. He was pleasant and wanted to know about the community, so I offered to show him around while he was there. He had a tight schedule, so we made a quick trip around, then back to the airstrip and he took off for his next destination.

Maree Manly

Dick Smith's visit with Terry Taylow

Dick's helicopter

The joys of being in a remote area once again affects all aspects of life. Life was hot….all work and no play. Some events were joyous, such as a marriage between staff. Our office administration officer Tim Nicholls met and fell in love with a nurse and they had a wonderful marriage ceremony. I was privileged to make the two heart-shaped cakes and decorate the tables. The pastor who officiated flew in from Mt Isa and the wedding and food were great. As it was the first staff wedding, we all felt that it was special.

CHAPTER 4

To say that life was interesting some days was an understatement. On one particular day, I noticed people running past my office, heading west towards the river. By the time I reached the scene, the elder ladies who led the pack were shouting at the driver of the grader, who was Rodney O'Keefe. He jumped down from the vehicle and told the elders to be quiet! They hushed up long enough for it to become clear that they thought that he was going to run the grader over the bower of a Bower bird that had been there for years! Rodney could not believe that they would think that he would run over the bower! He berated them, reminding them that he had known it was there since he was a boy. Two of the elder women apologised to Rodney and everyone went back to the store!

Slaughterhouse

Piggery

When I came to Doomadgee, there were quite a few successful industries, such as the Butchery, piggery, bakery and cattle. Suddenly, stockmen were out of work, the piggery closed and the farmer who tended the pigs and the vegetables and orchard was out of a job. The two butchers were no longer needed and the bakery closed. To me and the rest of the community, it was seen as a mad decision and did not take into account the short and long-term effects it would have on the people. This led to problems in the store, no longer could we buy fresh vegetables and fruit, no more pork which we all loved! The price rose on all those items that had to be shipped from Mt Isa by road, then by air in the wet season. One year, when I was running the Aged Persons Hostel, the plane company charged me $75 freight on 5 pumpkins! We contacted the Minister for Aboriginal Affairs and she declared a state of emergency as we were isolated by the flood waters and the freight charges on fresh vegetables and fruit were impossible to meet.

The residents of the Hostel were well fed in these times. I made dampers as we had no bread and the elders loved damper covered in Golden Syrup for smoko. During my time there, I learnt to make the best dampers, overseen by one of the residents who made sure I did it the right way, however the residents always reminded me that there is nothing like a damper made on the coals of an open fire! As this was not possible in the Hostel, I often put a call out to the community, asking if they had a fire going would they cook a damper for the elders, and someone always did.

On pay nights I would often make pizzas for the kids who came to visit the elders to get away from the noise and sometimes fighting at home. I loved to do this as the children were great company, full of stories and songs!

The visit each year by Fred Brophy's Boxing Troupe was a highlight enjoyed by adults and children alike. Some of the men thought they could beat the boxers, and when Fred used his megaphone to call them up, there was always a rush to be first in line. Needless to say they rarely won, but it was all good fun and broke the monotony of life in a remote community.

Fred Brophy's visit

Another group who came to give a concert every year was the band Coloured Stones. The children and teens loved them and danced and sang till the small hours. Another visitor was Les Hiddins, the Bush Tucker Man! He came through on his way to collect ideas for his Bush Tucker Map. It proved to be popular with travellers and those interested in what they could find and eat in the bush.

Another visitor was Father Crowley, who was invited to hold Mass in the home of one of the teachers. There were quite a few Catholics among the teachers, admin and nursing staff. What we were not prepared for was the reaction from the resident Pastor Doug Jones to Father Crowley's visit. His opinion was that we should have been practising the Exclusive Brethren's religion, not allowing any other church representatives to visit Doomadgee! We thought those days were gone. While we were attending Mass, the Pastor filled the back seat of Father Crowley's car with crudely drawn comics depicting nuns and priests having sex, nuns having babies and other awful cartoons related to anything Catholic! Father Crowley was so disgusted by this event that he left early to go back too Burketown, then on to Cairns. This behaviour by Pastor Jones was met with disgust by all the staff who attended Mass. I advised the Chairman, Wilfred Walden, who reacted by putting a notice on the board in front of the store apologising for Pastor Jones' behaviour and assuring the community that everyone was welcome to visit Doomadgee, no matter who they were, religious or otherwise!

Our admin staff were shocked by what had happened and we all felt that the Pastor has opened a wound that would not heal anytime soon. My own feeling was that those days of the church running everything had gone and this was so shocking that I could not bring myself to acknowledge him for a long time. It saddened me to know that such an awful religion had controlled the people of Doomadgee for 43 years and the damage they had done.

I also discovered that the missionary nurses gave the women and young girls Vitamin K injections that were really Deprovera, an injection to prevent pregnancy! Some people saw this as a good thing, to stop young girls having babies, however my point is that it was done without the permission of the women and girls. If that were done today, there would be a huge outcry about the violation of women's rights to choose. These tactics were used by missionaries around the world and was done with the best intentions, but in the case of Doomadgee, the effects are still being felt today! The issue of children being taken from their parents and placed in dormitories has created a generation of parents who do not know how to parent their children, causing a flow-on effect in the community.

During my time in Doomadgee, education was not ideal, but the teachers and principal did the best they could with what they had. There was a problem with children not attending school, so the principal at the time used the school bus to pick the kids up. This worked for a time, then breakfasts were introduced to encourage the kids to eat before school. I admired those mothers who volunteered to help with the breakfasts and see that everyone was fed. A good breakfast helped the kids study and listen. A problem for the school was the heat, it was intense at times, 40 – 45 degrees some days and the school was not air-conditioned in those days. School was sometimes closed early to allow the kids to go home!

Some teachers who came to Doomadgee were keen to teach but others were only there because they were sent to do 'rural service', and it showed! They did not join in community activities and could not wait to leave. Other teachers made the effort to settle into life in the town and tried to involve the parents and grandparents in the school life. There were many misconceptions held by teachers, such as Aboriginal children could not be taught basic maths. When I heard this, I assured the teachers involved that if they went down to the community on a pay night and visited the gambling ring, they would see children, whose parents were playing 21, (a gambling card game), adding up their parents' cards in their heads faster than their parents could. So much for kids not being able to do basic maths!

While I am on the subject of gambling, it was and still is a problem in remote communities like Doomadgee. A lot of money could be won and lost in a card game, but when you look at the history of Doomadgee, 43 years of oppression by the missionaries, isolation, and lack of worthwhile employment, you can understand how gambling can flourish.

New Council offices

Council was taking over more and more responsibility as each year passed and residents became more involved. It has to be remembered that these people had been controlled for years and had no experience at running a community. They did a good job and got better as each new council was elected. Clara Foster was the first woman to be elected to council and was a respected member of the community and a role model for the women and girls. She showed what could be achieved by an aboriginal woman in her community. Clara was always kind to me in my years in Doomadgee and I looked to her for guidance in all matters of the council and community. Clara had a large extended family that she enjoyed, especially her grandchildren.

When I was working at the Aged Persons Hostel, the residents included Eva Gilbert, who was a delight to care for, she was what I call a 'lady'. Like Clara Foster, she had an air about her. They carried themselves in an almost regal manner! Eva was the sister of the famous aboriginal cricketer, Eddie Gilbert, and spoke often of her regret that they were separated and did not keep in touch.

I enjoyed my time at the Hostel except for a problem with the alarm system which never worked, so we relied on people calling out to the staff if they needed help.

Dogs were a problem in the community, but on the whole they were kept in check by the owners. The use of 1080 baits by council was a real threat to all animals, but especially local dogs. The crows would drop the baits into the community and the dogs would pick them up. The stockman lost two of his best dogs with baits, having to shoot them to put them out of their misery. I was in my office one day when one of the council workers rushed in to tell me that my dog, Fergie, had taken a bait. I rushed home to find Fergie on her run under the house, watching a local dog running around my yard, foaming at the mouth. The poor thing was going crazy. The resident who owned the dog came and took it after it died, then I had the awful job of cleaning up all the foam from around my yard as it was the poison from the bait. The use of 1080 baits is a way of controlling pests such as wild dogs but the cost to domestic dogs is high and they die a terrible and agonizing death.

The wildlife around Doomadgee included introduced species such as buffalo, donkeys, cats, pigs, horses and camels. We had a resident donkey that used to sometimes sleep in the diesel generator shed. One morning as I was on my way to work, I was walking past the shed when the donkey poked his head out and frightened the life out of me. I must have jumped three feet in the air, but he just heehawed and grinned at me!

Donkey at the diesel shed

One of the joys of living in a remote community was that you make your own entertainment. Fishing was my passion, and along with yabbying, gave me a great release from the pressures of work. I would put my yabby log down every Friday night. It was a log with a tin plate at one end and wire netting at the other end. I would put meat at the end to attract the yabbies, then they would go in to get the meat and get tangled in the wire netting, unable to get out. There is nothing better than curried yabby with damper!

CHAPTER 5

Getting ill in a remote community was a constant fear of mine and I did become ill with Chronic Fatigue Syndrome. I spent a month in Mt Isa hospital, time that I remember little of as I spent most of the month sleeping. The staff only woke me to eat and shower. However, I do remember how kind they were to me. It took me two years to completely recover from that illness. I was later transported to Mt Isa again by the Flying Doctor to have my gall bladder removed. It took me a couple of months to recover then, but I had to go straight back to work. That was an experience!

Locals who became ill would be taken to Mt Isa but mothers who were pregnant had to go 6 weeks before their due date and stay until their baby was born. This put a huge strain on the fathers and other family members who had to care for the children left behind. It was no picnic for the mothers as they had little or no family support in Mt Isa, and often fretted about leaving their families. Some mothers were known to hide out till the baby was coming then the Flying Doctor had to be called to attend to the delivery in Doomadgee. Babies born in Mt Isa were not considered to be on country therefore it was against the custom of the people.

Illness such as leprosy was still common but treatable. It was sicknesses such as STDs that were causing a bigger problem. It was hoped that, with education, the rate of STDs would be controlled. This problem is not isolated to remote communities, a lot of STDs are seen in the cities as well as measles and Chicken Pox. One thing I must say about the nursing staff during my time is that they introduced clinics for vaccinations and sexual health education.

Gregory Downs canoe races were always popular and a great way to meet people of all kinds, graziers, nurses, police, public servants and visitors came from all over the west to take part in this special event.

Rodeos held in Doomadgee were always a reason to get down and dusty! The whole community would turn out to see would-be cowboys tossed off the bucking horses and bulls. There were some really good riders as well, so everyone was assured of an exciting time.

Funerals were the saddest times when I was in Doomadgee. The community would go into mourning for a long time, depending on who had passed away. People would travel vast distances to attend a funeral, not only in Doomadgee but in other areas as well, such as Borroloola and Mt Isa. The sense of grief was almost palpable if it was a young person or an elder. The relatives would hold a smoking ceremony in the deceased person's house. This was also done in the old First Aid Station when a baby was born. Their beliefs seemed to help the relatives cope with death and birth. I always found this style of ceremony very moving and spiritual. Everyone has their own beliefs, and if the smoking ceremonies help with the grieving process, then that is a good thing.

I cannot write about my time in Doomadgee without mentioning alcohol and drugs. Like all communities, these created a problem in how the people handle such issues. Under the Exclusive Brethren control, no alcohol or tobacco was allowed, except for chewing tobacco for the elders. Therefore, it was no surprise to me when illegal drugs and alcohol became an issue. Prohibition has never worked anywhere in the world, so to ban alcohol was not going to work in Doomadgee and still does not work today. Alcohol is sold at exorbitant prices during the wet season when the roads are closed, so people make a lot of money running alcohol between Burketown and Doomadgee. I have even seen boats being used to ferry grog across the flooded river!

The best Christmas I had in Doomadgee was when the roads were closed due to the wet and planes could not land. The community almost held their breath because it meant we could celebrate without the fights associated with grog. We played games such as broom throwing and cricket and had a Santa, which the kids loved. It was so peaceful.

Christmas was a time when we were made aware of just how isolated we were. The nearest shops were 500kms away so if anyone went to Mt Isa, they were always given a list of goods to bring back. The government-run store in Doomadgee stocked very few toys! The supply of food in the store was always a problem, and during the wet it was exacerbated as items such as milk, bread, fresh fruit and vegetables were in short supply. When they were available, they were seldom fresh!

The soil in Doomadgee was so rich that anything would grow in abundance, such as watermelons, potatoes, pumpkins, fruit trees and rock melons. However, when the orchard was closed and the farmer dismissed, all that ceased. There has always been the opportunity to start a garden again, it just needs funding. It would create jobs and the community would be assured of a supply of fresh food, especially during the wet season.

When I arrived in Doomadgee in 1986, there was out-of-date food in the store, especially milk that had been frozen, then defrosted! I put this down to the store manager trying to keep supplies up during the wet, but things have changed now. The store is still an important service to the community and it provides jobs for the residents.

Another issue, particularly during the wet season, was the freshwater crocodiles. I was never scared of them, they seemed more scared of us and took off as soon as we came near them in the water. I saw quite a few big 10 footers sunbaking on the Nicholson River banks. It always amazed me that the children would swim in the river with the freshwater crocodiles, snakes and turtles without any sense of fear!

CHAPTER 6

I have so many personal stories that I could write, about people who were important to me at the time, but I have chosen just one. The story is about Patsy O'Keefe, who worked in our Department office and became a close personal friend to me, and remains so today. She refers to me as "Sister from another mother"! I relate the story of Patsy's life in Doomadgee with her permission.

Patsy was born in Burketown, one of a family of 6 children. Her parents were drinkers and gamblers, so they were sent to Mornington Island to live when Patsy was 6 years of age and returned to Burketown when Patsy was about 12 or 13. While there, her father won some money on the Golden Casket. Her mother, father and the children were all under the Aboriginal Act, which her father resented and he was often punished for breaking the rules. The missionaries were complicit with the Queensland Government in all that happened in Doomadgee. Patsy's father had a child with another woman and this caused conflict, but Patsy has contact with her half-sister, Florence. (Because everyone was under the Act, it was easy for the missionaries to control the people. The Act dictated how everyone who lived on missions and in towns were to behave. The Act was administered in some towns, such as Burketown, by the Police.) Patsy met her future husband, Rodney O'Keefe, in Burketown. However, when she was 14 she was sent to Brisbane to be a housemaid with a family. Patsy states that they were good to her. She saw a different kind of lifestyle and was impressed by the freedom the young girls had compared to that of the girls in Burketown and Doomadgee. During the time she was in Brisbane, Patsy and Rodney wrote to each other for years. On her return, she stayed with her family in Doomadgee and met up with Rodney again.

The Pastor was aware of their relationship and insisted that they go down to the basketball courts and sit on a blanket under the lights so that the whole community could see that they were a couple. Rodney was not keen to do this but went along with it.

The Pastor married them in an old building down in the village when Patsy was 19 and Rodney 26. Patsy felt pressured into it, as her life's aim was not to get married and have children. She had experienced another lifestyle in Brisbane and she felt that she deserved a better chance at life. It was normal practice for the missionaries to marry the young ones despite their objections. This resonates in the community today as this type of marriage seldom lasted. The ones that did survive like that of Patsy and Rodney did so because there was a connection from the start. Many other arranged marriages were doomed, which seemed part and parcel of the missionaries' agenda.

Patsy said that her future mother-in-law came to see her parents with a fighting stick as she disapproved of Patsy but over time she accepted their relationship, especially when their three daughters came along. Patsy is a grandmother to 15 children and has worked for the Save the Children organisation.

An interesting individual who assisted the people of Doomadgee was Gordon Tait. Gordon lived across the river and owned a plane, which he used to transport people and goods to and from Doomadgee and Mt Isa. Gordon only charged a minimum of what the other airlines charged for these trips. I had reason to use Gordon's service when my dog, Fergie, became ill and had to be taken to the vet in Mt Isa. Gordon also picked her up and brought her home for me, as the other airlines would no longer take animals, so I was very grateful to Gordon and his service!

Gordon's plane

The two main languages spoken in Doomadgee were Gungalinda and Waanya. Booraloola had 5 different language groups as they had a mixture of people who came from all around the Northern Territory and Queensland. The elders of Doomadgee still spoke the languages and followed the old ways, despite the Exclusive Brethren's influence.

The building used as a guest house today used to be the home of Pastor Alan Hockey. In front of the house was a post used for whipping. The people who ran away or disobeyed the rules of the Pastor were whipped as punishment. Their hands were tied above their heads and they were whipped according to their transgression. One woman was asked to plant pumpkin seeds, but she did not want to so she threw them in a corner of the paddock. To her surprise, they all came up! The Pastor was upset with her so she was whipped. This type of punishment was harsh and was practised by a lot of missionaries throughout the world and was done in the name of God!

DC3 landing

When the old DC3 planes were no longer used to transport people and goods to Doomadgee and Flight West took over, it was as if we were given a terrific present! We could now have Fried Chicken or pizzas brought in for our special dinners. What a treat! Usually this happened when we showed films on the wall of the Council building. Everyone brought their food, chairs and blankets to sit on. Most families brought a bucket of the chicken which was enough for their whole family. The films were borrowed from the Education department and were a big hit with everyone. (I must add that the pilots of the Flight West planes were not as happy, as the smell of the chicken was quite overpowering!) These movie nights were a great way for the people to socialize in a relaxed setting.

Another activity was the fun runs for all ages, run by the Doomadgee teachers and the Police from Burketown. These were held early in the morning before the heat came and were enjoyed by all who took part. They were great levellers as the participants were so competitive!

Sport played a big part in everyday life in Doomadgee, especially football, cricket and netball. The one aspect of sport that stood out to me was that there were two sides of teams, one for the full-bloods and one for the creamy fellas. (The community's words, not mine!) There was fierce rivalry with a full-bloods cricket team and a creamy fellas football team. Both teams were very successful and travelled to Mt Isa and other towns to play their chosen sport. The girls' teams travelled away too and were also very dedicated and successful. It must be noted that the full-bloods and creamy fellas rarely played each other. This type of racism was practised by both sides and led to fights but were often resolved pretty quickly.

Regarding feuds and family discord, during my time these were settled in the paddock in the community. If it involved two young girls or boys, they fought it out, mostly slapping and punching till it was declared a draw or someone won. They were then made to shake hands and that had to be the end of it. It worked to a degree, but if it was family against family that could not be resolved by shaking hands, it sometimes went on for quite a while, as it does in most families, black or white.

Men's and women's business, such as initiations, were practised spasmodically. Men took the young boys out bush and the grandmothers took the young girls. What they did or learned I was not privy to, which is as it should be. Once again, it showed that the missionaries failed to wipe out their traditions and customs.

Another aspect of life was story telling. The women were great story tellers with words and physical actions. I have been so caught up in a story that I believed it! As an example, I was camped out bush with a group of women and children one weekend and as we were sitting around the fire that night, the women told me about the "Little people". I asked who were the Little people, and was told that they came into the camp while everyone was asleep, removed the lids off the Golden Syrup and put their fingers into the tin, then they would leave the lids off so you would know they've been. Of course, the next morning, the lids were off the tins and there was a mark in the syrup. The logical explanation was that the heat from the fire caused the lids to come off and leave a dimple in the syrup, but I like their explanation better.......don't you?

Another story that always intrigued me was that, if you heard the call of a goat, it meant that the Kadachi Man had been into the community, but as he wore feathered shoes, he left no footprints. In my time at Doomadgee, I never heard the call of a goat so I cannot say if the Kadachi Man ever visited. It comes down to what you wish to believe and how strongly.

The use of solar was introduced and was successful in that it was cheaper. Housing continues to be seen as a priority as families expand and the needs of the residents continue to change. The housing designs have changed over the years and they are Prefab now and easier to construct. In my early days in Doomadgee, there was an effort to train apprentices. Those wanting to learn a trade were sent to Mt Isa for theory and did their practical at home. I am not sure if this is still happening, but I hope it is, so the young people can be employed in Doomadgee.

Looking back on my time in Doomadgee, I saw the community change from a restricted, oppressed society into a community that was in charge of its own destiny, with a progressive council working with the Department to create a more sustainable lifestyle for its people. I watched as people became workers in their own community instead of being sent out to work on stations. The men were employed by Council as grader drivers, truck drivers and labourers. Women were employed at the store, hospital, council, Aboriginal Health, school and kindergarten. The future for Doomadgee lies in the hands of the Council. Their future responsibility is to guide the residents to become more self-sufficient and independent.

The End.

the Department of... give more confidence to their parents if pupils of
whom... would be dull students in their environment, represented
a fine... and himself to speakers. He made other explanations, mostly
suggestive of what loves a Watcher's... We have experienced it
this week. August arrived along, and again, It never added fittings, for
the future key to make him in the hands of the... it. This failure,
respectability is to guide this is able to be to be... more attention in
an advanced to...

Maree Manly

Maree Manly

Milton Keynes UK
Ingram Content Group UK Ltd.
UKHW021919151124
451262UK00014B/1487